Saving Turtles

A Kid's Guide to Helping Endangered Creatures

Sue Carstairs

FIREFLY BOOKS

A FIREFLY BOOK

Published by Firefly Books Ltd. 2014
Copyright © 2014 Firefly Books Ltd.
Text copyright © 2014 Sue Carstairs

First Printing

Publisher Cataloging-in-Publication Data (U.S.)
Carstairs Sue.
  Saving turtles : a kid's guide to helping endangered creatures / Sue Carstairs.
[64] pages : color photos. ; cm.
Includes index.
Summary: Kids' guide to turtle conservation, and how turtles can continue to survive in our world.
ISBN-13: 978-1-77085-434-5
ISBN-13: 978-1-77085-290-7 (pbk.)
1. Turtles — Juvenile literature.
2. Turtles — Conservation — Juvenile literature. 3. Endangered species — Juvenile literature. I. Title.
597.92 dc23   QL666.C5C3678 2014

Library and Archives Canada Cataloguing in Publication
Carstairs, Sue, 1961–, author
  Saving turtles : a kid's guide to helping endangered creatures / Sue Carstairs.
Includes index.
ISBN 978-1-77085-434-5 (bound).
ISBN 978-1-77085-290-7 (pbk.)
  1. Turtles — Juvenile literature.
2. Turtles — Conservation — Juvenile literature.   I. Title.
QL666.C5C37 2014
j597.92   C2014-901157-1

Published in the United States by
Firefly Books (U.S.) Inc.
P.O. Box 1338, Ellicott Station
Buffalo, New York 14205

Published in Canada by
Firefly Books Ltd.
50 Staples Avenue, Unit 1
Richmond Hill, Ontario L4B 0A7

Cover and interior design: LINDdesign
Illustrations: Nick Craine

Printed in China

The publisher gratefully acknowledges the financial support for our publishing program by the Government of Canada through the Canada Book Fund as administered by the Department of Canadian Heritage.

Photo Credits

Cover: top: Shutterstock©Alexandra Lande; bottom left: Shutterstock©Roman Zherdytskyi; bottom right: Shutterstock©Jason Patrick Ross; bottom center: Shutterstock©Khoroshunova Olga
page 3: Shutterstock©Frank L. Junior
page 4: Michael Mouland
page 6–7: iStock©JaredAlden
page 8–9: Shutterstock©Randimal
page 10: Shutterstock©Jay Ondreicka
page 11: top left: Michael Mouland; bottom right: Shutterstock©Rich Carey; bottom left: Shutterstock©Africa Studio; top right: Shutterstock©David Evison; bottom center: Shutterstock©Tooykrub
page 13: Sue Carstairs
page 14: Shutterstock©Pablo Hidalgo
page 15: top left: Shutterstock©IrinaK; top right: National Geographic Image Collection/Joel Sartore; bottom left: Shutterstock©Lepas; bottom right: Shutterstock©IrinaK
page 16-17: Shutterstock©Maxim Blinkov
page 18: Dreamstime©Gow927
page 19: top right: Michael Mouland; bottom right: Sue Carstairs; bottom left: Shutterstock©Kletr; top left: National Geographic Image Collection/Joel Sartore
page 22: top & bottom right: Shutterstock©Rich Carey
page 22–23: Images 1–25 courtesy of Turtle Survival Alliance: #1: E.H. Chan; #2: C. Tabaka; #3: B.D. Horne; #4: R. Ghosh; #5: R. Hudson; #6: B.D. Horne; #7: T. Zhou, W.P. McCord, T. Blanck; #8: G. Kuchling; #9: T. Blanck; #10: P. Crow; #11: T. McCormack; #12: R.M. Brown; #13: C. Hagen; #14: A.G.J. Rhodin; #15: R. Reed; #16: G. Kuchling; #17: D. Hendrie; #18: T. Blanck; #19: A. de Villiers; #20: A.G.J. Rhodin; #21: A.G.J. Rhodin; #22: R.A. Mittermeier; #23: A.G.J. Rhodin; #24: A. Cadavid; #25: M. Merida
page 24: Shutterstock©Frank L. Junior
page 25: Michael Mouland
page 26: top and bottom left: Michael Mouland
page 27: Top left and right: Sue Carstairs; bottom: Michael Mouland
page 28: Michael Mouland
page 29: all photos: Michael Mouland
page 30: Sue Carstairs
page 31: all photos: Sue Carstairs
page 32: Shutterstock©Gerald A. DeBoer

page 33: all photos: Sue Carstairs
page 34–35: Sue Carstairs
page 36: top: Shutterstock©David Evison; bottom left: Michael Mouland
page 37: top three images: Michael Mouland; bottom right: Sue Carstairs
page 38: Sue Carstairs
page 39: top right: Sue Carstairs; bottom: Michael Mouland
page 40: Sue Carstairs
page 41: right and top left: Michael Mouland; bottom left: Sue Carstairs
page 42: Shutterstock©Polly Dawson
page 43: top: Shutterstock©Kjersti Joergensen; middle right: Shutterstock©Matt Jeppson; bottom left: Shutterstock©Jorg Hackemann; bottom right: Shutterstock©StacieStauffSmith Photos
page 44: Shutterstock©Wichan Kongchan
page 45: Sue Carstairs
page 46: Sue Carstairs
page 47: top left: Sue Carstairs; top right: National Geographic Image Collection/ Joel Sartore; bottom left and right: Sue Carstairs
page 48: Shutterstock©Matt Jeppson
page 49: top left & right: Sue Carstairs; bottom right: Juan Manuel Vargas-Ramirez
page 50: top: Sue Carstairs; left bottom: B.D. Horne/Turtle Survival Alliance
page 51: top left: E.H. Chan/Turtle Survival Alliance; top right: Shutterstock©Jacqui Martin
page 52: Shutterstock©XiXinXing
page 53: iStock©kali9
page 54: Sue Carstairs
page 55: top and bottom: Sue Carstairs
page 56: main and inset: Sue Carstairs
page 57: top left and inset: Sue Carstairs; top right: Shutterstock©Pierre-Yves Babelon; bottom: A. Cadavid/Turtle Survival Alliance
page 58–59: Shutterstock©My Good Images
page 60: Sue Carstairs
page 61: top left: Shutterstock©jam4travel; top right: Sue Carstairs

Contents

Here, a new admission is assessed and a surgical plan put into place. With Sue Carstairs, the author (right), is Jennifer, a volunteer with the centre, whose regular job is emergency medicine in humans!

A Note from the Author

When I graduated from veterinary school, my goal was to work in wildlife conservation, combining medicine with conservation. Although I enjoy helping with all wildlife, my work with turtles is perfect for me, as it combines medicine and conservation so well. Turtles are in trouble all over the world. In Ontario alone, seven of the eight species are listed as "at risk." Through the past 200 million years, turtles have survived with little change, and with the same life history. To ensure the continuation of healthy species, they rely on a long life and very low adult mortality. These days, not many eggs make it to hatching, let alone to adulthood! Turtles also take a long time to mature, and it therefore takes a long time to replace a lost adult. As a result, populations cannot tolerate the loss of adults that is being experienced by species around the world—through habitat loss, road and fishing mortalities, pollution and illegal harvesting. The Ontario Turtle Conservation Centre (OTTC, previously the Kawartha Turtle Trauma Centre) was established as a registered charity in 2002. Although it started as a hospital to treat injured native Ontario turtles and release them back into the wild, it now has an even broader impact on turtle conservation. We developed an extensive hatchling program and are now also conducting a lot of field work. Education is a key to all areas, as getting the public involved is essential to creating change.

I joined the centre in 2009 and am currently the executive and medical director. It really is the most amazing project, and our work is making an impact. I feel very lucky to be a part of it, and look forward to seeing it develop even more. I hope you enjoy reading about our work, as well as the work of many tremendous turtle biologists throughout the world. Please see our website at www.kawarthaturtle.org to find out more and to learn how you can get involved.

—Sue Carstairs

Introduction

ave you ever seen a turtle? Maybe you've come across one in a rural area near your home, or at a wildlife center or conservation area. Even if you've never seen a turtle "in real life," you probably know a few things about them: they have shells (and most can hide their heads inside them); they move slowly; they are cold-blooded reptiles; they can live for a long, long time.

But there are many amazing things about turtles that you probably don't know. For example, turtles have been around for 220 million years—longer than the dinosaurs—and research tells us they haven't changed much since those prehistoric times. Small turtles can live as long as 50 years, while tortoises and sea turtles can live 100 years or longer. Turtles have no teeth and can't chew, which means they have to use other tools to help them eat. During the spring, summer and fall, they live and breathe the way humans do, with their lungs. But in the colder winter months, they can burrow into the mud at the bottom of a lake and hibernate, getting their oxygen in a different way.

There's a lot more that we can learn about and from turtles, but time may be running out. Of the roughly 300 species of turtles that exist today, more than half are threatened with extinction, making turtles one of the most endangered vertebrates in the world. Freshwater, marine and land turtles are all affected. What's threatening this amazing species? We are! As the human race grows and takes up more space on the planet, turtles are losing their homes, suffering from the effects of pollution and being sought out as pets and food. They are killed by trucks and cars as they try to cross roads, and they are snared in fishing nets meant to catch other species. Very few of the eggs turtles lay survive to maturity. The future looks bleak.

Thankfully, a community of scientists, environmentalists and concerned citizens has come together to help. All around the world, efforts are underway to protect and save turtles. In this book, you'll meet some of those people and learn about their work in education, rehabilitation and research. And you'll discover what you can do to help. But first, let's learn more about turtles.

Dangerous road crossings are just one of the many threats facing turtles around the world.

Chapter 1
Getting to Know Turtles

urtles are fascinating creatures. Their anatomy and physiology is unique, but their basic "design" has been the same for more than 200 million years. (It's obviously successful!) Turtles are totally harmless, which is probably one of the main reasons they are loved all around the world. They are a vital part of the habitat in which they live—wherever they live—and are an essential part of healthy wetlands, lakes, rivers, oceans and land.

Turtles basking in the sun—a favorite activity.

Turtle Facts and Figures

Freshwater turtles tend to be semi-aquatic, meaning they live on the land and in the water.

Habitat

Turtles live all over the world. Some spend most of their time in oceans, lakes and rivers. Others live on the land, in forests and in deserts. Still others are semi-aquatic—which means they divide their time between the water and the land. These turtles can be found in bogs, swamps, marshes and wetlands. Turtles do not live in the Artic or Antarctica.

Changing Seasons, Changing Habits

All turtles are ectotherms, or "cold-blooded." This means that turtles depend on the environment to maintain their body temperature, as they cannot regulate it on their own. Different types of turtles manage this issue in different ways.

Turtles that live in cold climates hibernate during the winter season. In late fall, they slow down and seek out their hibernation sites under the ice of lakes and streams.

Left: The Ontario Turtle Conservation Centre uses lots of worms! Right: This marine turtle is laying eggs in a hole she has dug on the beach. The eggs are laid at night.

Turtles that live in hot, dry climates also burrow underground, but they do so to escape the hottest months of year. This activity is called estivation.

Diet

Most turtles eat plants, insects, fish, amphibians, small birds and small mammals. A sea turtle's diet includes algae, seagrass, crabs and jellyfish. How much and how often turtles eat depends on the species, but because of their very slow metabolism, they can go much longer without eating than birds or mammals. Some can go weeks without food and not lose any weight!

Reproduction

All species of turtles lay eggs on dry land. Even sea turtles, which spend their lives in the water, will come ashore to lay their eggs.

Some turtles lay their eggs in piles of leaves or in a thin layer of soil, but most turtles prefer to leave their eggs in a specially prepared nest. Once the eggs are laid, the turtle covers them and leaves. The number of eggs a female turtle lays varies widely by species. Some lay just two or three, while others can lay a hundred or more.

Turtles, Tortoises and Terrapins

Turtles belong to the *chelonia* order of shelled reptiles, as do tortoises and terrapins. What's the difference? The terminology changes depending on where you live. In North America, the word *turtle* generally refers to any reptile with a shell. However, turtles that live only on land are called *tortoises*. In other parts of the world, tortoises live on land, *terrapins* are semi-aquatic and live in freshwater and *turtle* refers to species that live in salt water. No matter what you call them, they're all chelonians!

Some turtles live on land and in water.

Tortoises live only on land.

Marine turtles live in salt water.

Anatomy of a Turtle

Shell (carapace and plastron)

The top part of a turtle's shell is called the carapace, and the bottom part is the plastron. These are connected along the sides of the turtle, forming the shell compartment.

Inside the shell compartment are the turtle's internal organs, including the lungs. Because the turtle's shell is hard, its chest cavity can't expand and contract as the turtle breathes. It has to push air in and out of its lungs another way—by using strong trunk muscles that expand and contract the lungs with their movement. If you've ever picked up a turtle, you may have heard a hissing noise. That's the sound of air being quickly pushed out of the lungs to make room for the head under the shell.

Some species, such as box turtles and Blanding's turtles, have hinges of flexible tissue between the bony plates of the plastron. This allows them to close up the shell like a box, providing added protection.

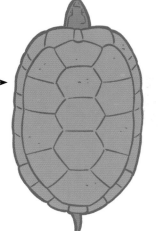

Carapace (top)

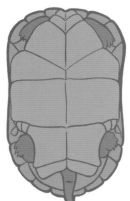
Plastron (bottom)

Eye

Turtles see in color, and they use their eyesight and sense of smell to find food. In marine turtles, the tear duct is modified into a gland that helps to expel excess salt from the body. When that happens, it can look as if the turtle is crying.

Gall bladder

Stomach

Liver

Heart

Beak

Turtles do not have teeth. Since they cannot chew, they use their sharp beaks and claws to tear off bite-sized pieces of food. Turtles eat plants, insects, fish, small birds, amphibians and small mammals.

Feet

Most turtles are pigeon-toed. That means they walk with their feet turned inward. Aquatic turtles have webbed toes, and long, sharp claws. Turtles that live on the land have shorter toes, better suited for digging.

Lungs

The lungs sit just underneath the carapace. Often when turtles injure their shell, this will lead to damage to the lungs too. Turtles have no diaphragm, however, and so can still breath even with an injury into the lungs

Scutes

A turtle's shell is covered with horny plates called scutes. Scutes are made of living tissue and contain nerve endings, which means that a turtle can feel when something touches its shell. Scutes feature colors and patterns that are distinct to each species. The sea turtle's scutes were once such a popular material for jewelry and other decorative items that the species was nearly hunted into extinction.

Skin and Bones

Many people don't realize that the turtle's shell is actually made of bone covered by a modified skin. Their ribs and vertebrae are fused into a boney plate that makes up the carapace. This means that when they injure or crack the shell, it is just like breaking a bone—and just as painful! The lower shell is formed similarly and is also made of bone covered by a modified skin. The skin has sensation, just as ours does.

Testes

GI tract (intestines)

Urinary bladder

Vent

The vent is a single opening under the tail for the turtle's digestive, urinary, and reproductive tracts. The **cloaca** (not shown) is a vestibule inside the turtle where the gastrointestinal, urinary and reproductive tracts empty into. These products then exit the body via the vent.

Amazing Turtles

ig turtles and small turtles. Marine turtles and turtles that live on land. Rare turtles and common turtles. Here are some of the most amazing turtles in the world.

Oldest

Although it's difficult to accurately guess a turtle's age, Lonesome George was one of the oldest. When he died in 2012, scientists estimated that he was more than 100 years old. He was also the last of his species—the Pinta Island tortoise (the island of Pinta is in the northern regions of the Galapagos archipelago). An inscription outside Lonesome George's old enclosure reads: "Whatever happens to this single animal, let him always remind us that the fate of all living things on Earth is in human hands."

Rarest

There are several critically endangered turtle species in the world, but the Red River giant softshell turtle is perhaps the most threatened of all. This amazing turtle can reach a whopping 250 pounds (113 kg). There are now only four in the world. One has lived for decades in Hoan Kiem Lake in downtown Hanoi, Vietnam, and is respected and worshipped by locals. Another lives in a nearby lake. Both are males. The other two—a male and a female—live in China's Suzhou Zoo. They used to live in separate enclosures, but thanks to the work of conservation groups, they now live together. However, the male is possibly 100 years old, and so far, no viable eggs have been produced.

Most Common

One of the world's most common turtles is the red-eared slider. This turtle does well almost everywhere and is extremely popular as a pet. Many were discarded into the wild when the people who'd bought them eventually found them too large or difficult to keep. They are one of the few turtles that don't seem to mind being relocated. While this is an interesting adaptation, it's also worrisome to biologists, since no one knows how the introduction of a new species will affect the existing populations.

Red-eared slider

Smallest

The speckled padloper tortoise, which lives in South Africa, is the smallest in the world. It reaches a length of only 3 inches (7.5 cm) and a weight of just 5 ounces (142 g).

Largest

The leatherback sea turtle is the largest living turtle. Surprisingly, they start out small (above), weighing just over an ounce when they hatch. By the time they mature, however, they can weigh between 550 and 1,500 pounds (250–680 kg), and stretch to between 6 and 7.2 feet (1.8–2.2 m) in length. They are considered critically endangered.

Chapter 2
The Turtle Crisis

Turtles are in crisis. Of the more than 300 species worldwide, about half are currently threatened with extinction. Freshwater, marine and land turtles are all affected. The situation in Asia—where nearly 80 percent of freshwater turtles have been lost in the past decade—is so serious that it even has a name: the Asian Turtle Crisis.

Faced with this dire situation, many governments, scientists and concerned individuals have come together to save the turtles. But in order for their efforts to succeed, people must first understand the problem. In this chapter, you'll learn how habitat loss, habitat fragmentation, pollution, harvesting for food and the pet trade, and road and fishing deaths continue to threaten turtles around the world. You'll also meet some of the most threatened turtles on the planet.

Pollution in the ocean poses a real threat to turtles.

Threats to Turtles

Cars

Road injuries and deaths are responsible for the loss of a great number of turtles. In many parts of the world, roads now run through traditional turtle habitats. In southern Ontario, for example, you cannot travel more than a mile without encountering a road. No wonder the turtles have a problem!

Boats

The large number of boats—in both fresh and salt water—make travel for turtles perilous. Unfortunately, many of the turtles injured in the water are never found, and therefore never treated.

Animals

Many animals feed on turtle eggs, and most turtle nests are dug up by predators before the eggs have a chance to hatch. Very young turtles are hunted by predators of all kinds, from birds to otters. Did you know that your family dog is also a predator? Dogs have been known to hunt turtles of all ages.

Habitat Loss/Fragmentation

Loss and disruption of habitat is the single worst threat to turtles today. It has the most influence on population declines, and is a worldwide problem. As wetlands are destroyed, roads built, and wild lands claimed by humans, the number of places that turtles can safely make their homes is fast decreasing.

Fishing

Fishing affects turtles in both the oceans and fresh waters. Although turtles are not often the target of the fishing, they can become a "bycatch" of the nets and hooks, leading to a number of unnecessary deaths.

Burmese star tortoise

Food Trade

Around the world, turtles of all life stages are harvested for food. From eggs to adults, they are collected in unsustainable numbers. In Ontario, the snapping turtle is still legally hunted for food, even though it is listed as a species at risk. In Myanmar, the Burmese star tortoise has been hunted to the point of near extinction.

Pet Trade

Many species of turtles are illegally collected from the wild and transported to other countries for sale as pets. This occurs all over the world. Unfortunately, the more endangered a turtle is, the greater the price to the poachers.

The puncture wounds in the top and bottom of this turtle's shell are the result of an attack by a dog.

Turtles are often brought in to treatment centers with injuries from fishing hooks.

Left: Is there construction near where you live? Think of all the wildlife that is being displaced as a result.

A Global Problem

The threat to turtles is a **global problem.** There is at least one endangered species on every continent except Antarctica (where turtles do not live).

Public education is always important, to teach people what they can do to protect their native turtles. You will learn more about some of these projects in chapter 6.

Pictured are the locations of the top 25 most endangered freshwater turtles and tortoises (see description, next page), along with the nesting sites of the marine turtle species (dark areas along shorelines).

North America

Marine turtles such as the leatherback nest on North American shores. They are considered critically endangered.

Galapagos

The Abington Island tortoise, found in the Galapagos in low numbers, is in grave danger.

South Asia

River terrapins are some of the most endangered turtles in the world. Conservation efforts are underway across Asia.

10,11, 15, 18

7, 8, 9, 10, 11, 18

3

10

3

4, 5, 6

2

1

17

12

1

2

1

13

14

Australia

The Mary River turtle and the Western Swamp turtle, both of which live in Australia, are among the most endangered fresh water turtles in the world.

16

21

20

19

Madagascar

The ploughshare tortoise is on the global "Top 25" list for endangered turtles.

Turtles in Trouble

Meet the 25 most endangered freshwater species on the planet:

1 Southern River Terrapin Cambodia, Indonesia, Malaysia

2 Asian Narrow-Headed Softshell Turtle Indonesia, Malaysia, Thailand

3 Red-Crowned Roofed Turtle Bangladesh, India, Nepal

4 Northern River Terrapin Bangladesh, India, Myanmar

5 Burmese Roofed Turtle Myanmar

6 Burmese Star Tortoise Myanmar

7 Yunnan Box Turtle China

8 Yellow-Headed Box Turtle China

9 McCord's Box Turtle China

10 Chinese Three-Striped Box Turtle China, Laos, Vietnam

11 Red River Giant Softshell Turtle China, Vietnam

12 Philippine Forest Turtle Philippines

13 Sulawesi Forest Turtle Indonesia

14 Roti Island Snake-Necked Turtle Indonesia

15 Vietnamese Pond Turtle Vietnam

16 Western Swamp Turtle Australia

17 Painted Terrapin Southeast Asia

18 Zhou's Box Turtle China, Vietnam

19 Geometric Tortoise South Africa

20 Madagascan Big-Headed Turtle Madagascar

21 Ploughshare Tortoise Madagascar

22 Hoge's Side-Necked Turtle Brazil

23 Pinta Island Giant Tortoise Now extinct (was in Galapagos)

24 Magdalena River Turtle Colombia

25 Central American River Turtle Central America

The hawksbill turtle is critically endangered.

Marine Turtle Troubles

Several species of marine turtles are facing extinction as well. Of the seven species of marine turtles, five are considered either endangered or critically endangered.

Endangered: green turtle (above), loggerhead turtle

Critically Endangered: hawksbill turtle, leatherback turtle and Kemp's ridley turtle

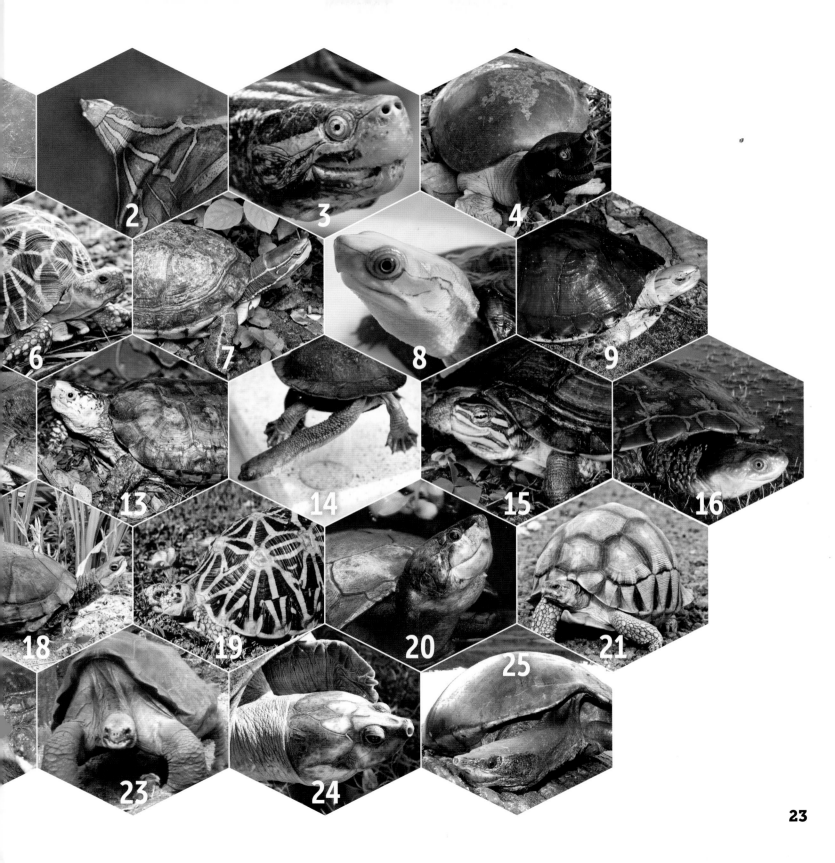

Chapter 3
Turtle Rescue and Rehabilitation

y now it should be clear why turtle rescue and rehabilitation is a necessity. If we don't do something to stop the many threats that turtles face, these amazing species will be extinct before we know it.

Rescue and rehabilitation efforts are taking place all over the world. Marine turtles are protected by organizations such as the Loggerhead Marinelife Center in Juno Beach, Florida. Turtle Survival Alliance India promotes stewardship of local species and teaches the public how to protect turtles. They are also active in conserving species through egg protection, "headstarting" and prevention of poaching. The Behler Chelonian Center in California concentrates on the breeding and maintenance of endangered species. In Canada, the Ontario Turtle Conservation Centre aids in the conservation of turtles and their habitats, and focuses on the rehabilitation of injured turtles. The combined efforts of such organizations are helping to turn the tide for turtles.

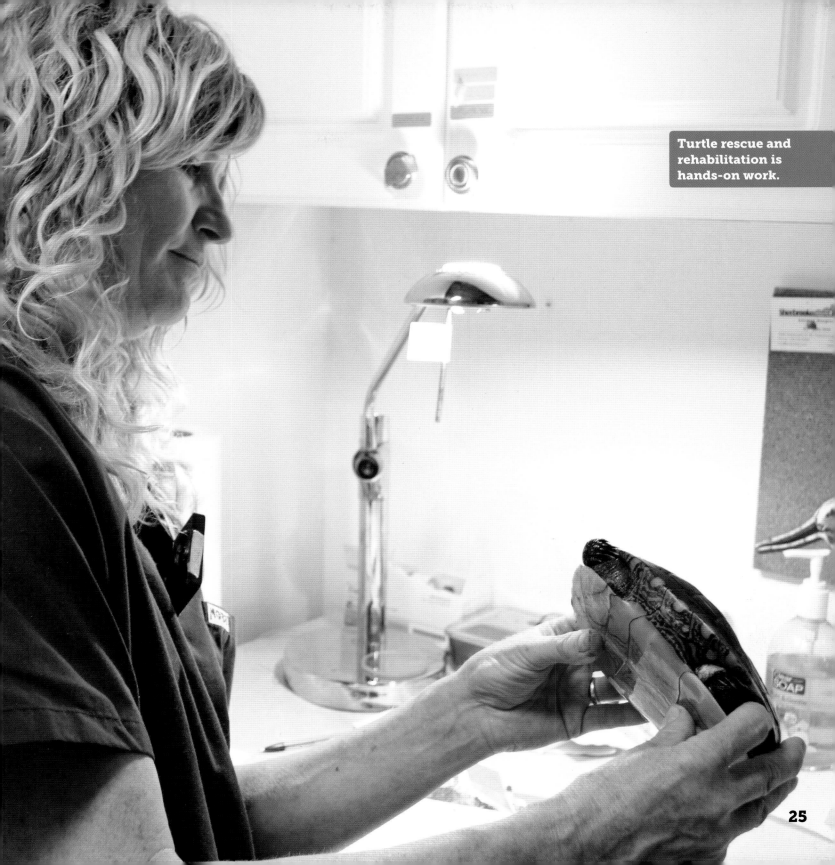

Turtle rescue and rehabilitation is hands-on work.

Treating Turtles

On busy days, the treatment board at a turtle trauma center can be crowded.

turtle rescue and rehabilitation center is an amazing place. At the Ontario Turtle Conservation Centre, for example, veterinarians, scientists, conservationists and volunteers all pitch in to help. From the moment an injured turtle is brought through the doors, it receives the highest level of care—and experiences some things that might surprise you!

Injured turtles are brought to the center by members of the public, biologists, other veterinarians and

rehabilitators, and via a network of "turtle taxi" volunteers.

The injured turtle is given a number and a medical record, and treatment is started right away. Often, the initial treatment needs to be done in stages, as the turtle needs pain medication before any invasive work is done. Some people think that just because turtles don't vocalize, they don't feel pain. This is not true! Scientists have found that turtles have the same pain tolerance as humans. All injured turtles that come to the OTCC receive

26

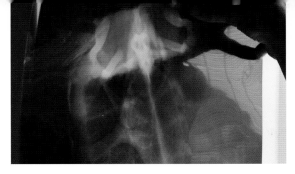
X-rays make it easier to understand the seriousness of a turtle's injury.

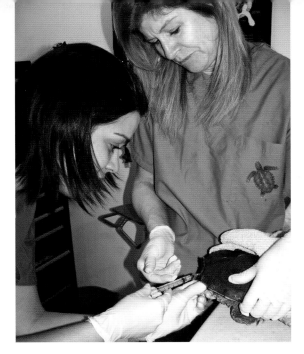
Blood work helps the trauma team track progress and recovery.

pain management. Fluid therapy is also essential, as the turtles are often in shock.

Many of the turtles brought into the trauma center have internal injuries that are not easy to identify by sight. In these cases, turtles have blood taken for analysis, and undergo X-rays. Not only do the X-rays show fractures, they also reveal if a turtle has eggs, and, if so, how many. This is important information, as the trauma team can then make sure that the eggs are laid while the turtle is in the hospital (see chapter 4 for more information).

Surgery takes place once the turtle is strong enough to endure an anesthetic. This might include having a fractured jaw wired, removing a fishing hook or wiring pieces of carapace back together.

All turtles have blood work done on admission and prior to release. This helps the team follow their progress and ensure they are on the right track for recovery.

Turtles are treated daily by a staff of veterinarians and veterinary technicians. This treatment can include fluid therapy, pain medication, antibiotic treatment and wound dressings. Treatments take an entire day to get through in the busy season.

Once fully healed, the turtle is released back to the body of water nearest to where it was found.

A tube is connected to an anesthetic machine that passes oxygen and anesthetic gas to the turtle. The surgery to repair this snapping turtle's facial trauma can now begin.

Shell Injuries

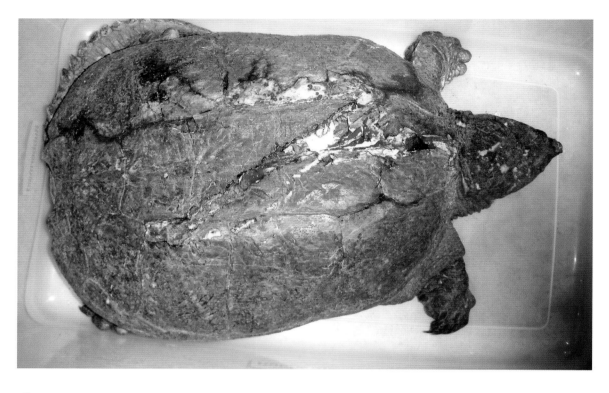

This snapping turtle has been injured by a boat propeller. This deep wound will take a long time to heal, but with intensive care, the carapace will repair and he will be released.

n chapter 1, we learned a bit about a turtle's shell. Not surprisingly, the health of the shell is key to a turtle's overall health. When the shell is cracked or damaged in any way, it's very painful (think of breaking one of your bones!) and very serious. A turtle cannot survive without its shell.

The most common injuries seen in smaller turtles involve fractures of the carapace. Sometimes, these fractures open right into the body cavity. Larger species, such as snapping turtles, are often brought to the center with very deep scratches along the carapace—an injury that occurs when cars try to "straddle" the turtles as they cross the road.

There are a number of ways to repair a damaged shell.

Wound Dressings

Some injuries are relatively minor and can be treated simply with bandages. The wounds need to be cleaned and then dressed carefully. Bandages must be changed regularly as the turtle heals.

Snapping turtles often get deep wounds into their carapace. Here, one of these wounds is being cleaned, and a dressing placed.

A wound dressing has been applied and a clear sticky covering is placed. This keeps the wound clean and dry, yet sticks to the shell so the turtle can go back into shallow water.

A Blanding's turtle with a dressed wound. This wound created a hole right into the body cavity. The wound has to be carefully cleaned and dressed daily with a sterile dressing to avoid infection.

Orthopedic Wire

When humans break or fracture bones, surgeons often use orthopedic wire to hold the injured pieces together so healing can begin. The same technique can work for turtles with injured shells.

Cable Ties

Cable ties are used for all sorts of things—to tie up garbage bags, to fasten plants to stakes in the garden and to hold loose items together. At a turtle rehabilitation center, cable ties bring fractures together on larger species of turtle such as Blanding's turtles and snapping turtles.

This Blanding's turtle is having a shell fracture repaired. Using a dental drill, a hole is drilled into the shell on either side of the fracture (1), and orthopedic wire is used to bring the two pieces securely together (2–3). This wire will stay on for many months.

Cable clips are attached to the shell with epoxy and a cable tie is fed through these. A second cable tie is then zipped onto the first and pulled tightly. This method is a great way to get the pieces of fracture together firmly without having to screw anything into the shell. Once healed, the cable clips can be popped off.

Other Injuries

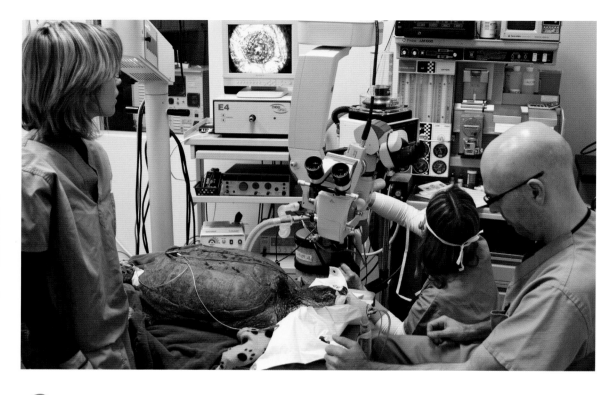

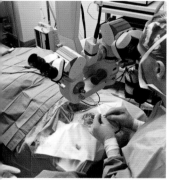

Many surgeries involve eyes. This large snapping turtle had only one eye, and it was blind due to a cataract. Dr. Joe Wolfer, a veterinary ophthalmologist, removed this cataract and restored sight to that eye. This turtle was successfully released.

Shells are not the only part of a turtle that is prone to damage. Other common injuries involve trauma to the head, including the jaws. Fractured jaws are particularly common in snapping turtles, and require surgery to wire the fractures back together. They tend to heal very well, however.

Head trauma is also common and can cause severe problems. Only time will tell if these injured turtles can regain the function that is required for a life in the wild.

Jaw Repair

Often, turtles will fracture their jaw when hit on the road. These fractures can involve the upper jaw (maxilla) or lower jaw (mandible). The fracture is repaired under anesthetic using orthopedic wire drilled into the jaw and secured on the outside.

Head Injuries

Head injures are very common in turtles hit on the road. This especially the case for snapping turtles, as they cannot pull their head into their

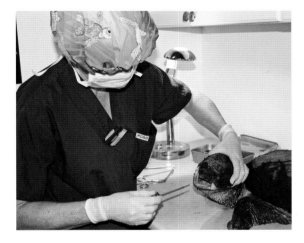

The orthopedic wire is placed around the jaw fracture, bringing the two pieces back together so the jaw can heal securely. This wire will be left in for the winter and removed in the spring prior to release. X-rays will be taken at that time to ensure that the bones have healed well.

shell as other turtles can. This leaves the head more exposed and vulnerable to trauma.

Eye Care

Turtles can suffer from the same eye problems as humans—cataracts, injury, blindness. When an injured turtle is brought into a center, the trauma team examines its eyes and fixes what can be fixed. It will be released only when the team is certain that it can see out of at least one eye.

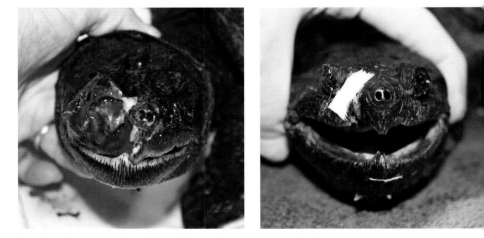

Head injuries can look horrific, but they often heal very well with proper medical care. If the pieces are too small to wire, or if wire cannot be placed in them, the fractured areas are sometimes replaced using surgical tape.

Healing and Release

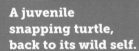t's probably no surprise that turtles are slow healers—after all, **they do everything slowly.** But turtles are also exceptionally good healers! They have an ability to heal by second intention. This means that even with very serious wounds—for example, where there aren't enough pieces of shell to put back together in surgery—proper care and good support allow the turtle's body to rebuild the site to close to the original state. This is an incredible process to watch. Given enough time, the great majority of these turtles can be released back into the wild.

Release

How long a turtle remains in the center depends on both the type of injury and when the injury occurred. Turtles admitted early in the season are ready to be released the same summer; others will need to remain in the center over the winter. But no matter how long a turtle stays in the hospital, its release must be carefully managed.

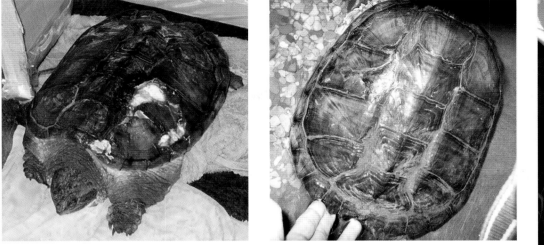

These photos illustrate the amazing ability of turtles to heal. Can you see where the wound was?

It's important for turtles to be returned to an area very close to where they were found, generally within half a mile. This is their home, and studies have shown that they will have the strongest chance at survival if they are released in a place that is familiar to them.

Different populations of turtles are genetically different, and it's important not to interfere with this natural diversity. Also, some populations may carry an infectious agent that does not cause its members any problem. When transferred to another population, however, that agent could cause harm.

During release, the turtle is placed in the nearest body of appropriate water, depending on the species. Some species like deep lakes, others prefer swampy wetlands.

A snapper (above) and a painted turtle (top right) being released after a stay in a trauma center.

Generally, even if a turtle has been treated for an extensive period of time at the hospital, as soon as they contact the water "back home" they submerge and swim off without even a thank you! Their old instincts quickly kick in, and they are back to their "wild" selves.

Chapter 4
Headstarting

great number of injuries and deaths occur when turtles are on their way to lay their eggs. In order to ensure that these eggs are not lost, many rescue and rehabilitation centers harvest, incubate, hatch and release the babies. This process is known as "headstarting."

A painted turtle gets ready to meet the world.

Harvesting

This turtle is digging a nest for her eggs.

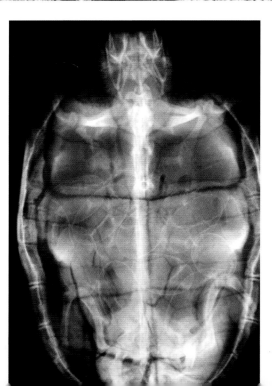

An X-ray of a gravid (egg-carrying) female. Once the eggs have a hard shell, they can be seen easily on X-rays.

urtle eggs can be collected in a number of different ways, depending on the health of the turtle. The first step, though, is often an X-ray to determine the number of eggs the female is carrying.

Nesting

If a female turtle is well enough, she can be encouraged to lay her eggs on her own. In the wild, turtles nest on dry land, although each species has its own preferences when it comes to how wet, dry, sandy or deep the nest

In the above series of photos, a Blanding's turtle has her eggs harvested. Unfortunately, she was dead when she was brought into the center. However, a technician was able to successfully harvest a clutch of healthy eggs.

should be. Many centers can provide smaller species with suitable material for a nest (finding enough space for larger species to lay eggs in captivity can be a challenge!). Left undisturbed, the turtles will often nest on their own and lay their eggs—which can then be harvested, counted, incubated and hatched.

This Blanding's turtle has been given a sandbox in which to lay her eggs. Once laid, the eggs can be collected for incubating.

Induction

If a turtle is too severely injured to nest on her own—contamination with sand or other materials can worsen wounds—she can be given a drug to "induce" the laying of eggs. This procedure uses the same drug that is used to encourage labor in humans! Every species is different in their reaction to induction, with some taking longer than others to respond. As with nesting, once the induced eggs are laid they are collected and counted before being incubated.

Egg Removal

Sometimes, a deceased female is brought in to a center, or perhaps a turtle dies shortly after arrival. Thankfully, her eggs can still be harvested surgically. This allows conservationists to ensure the continuation of the mother's genes.

Incubation

Once harvested, eggs are placed in a bed of moistened vermiculite.

Once the eggs have been **collected, they are placed in a container with moistened vermiculite.** This is the same material that is used for potting plants; it is also used in egg incubations for many species. Vermiculite holds on to moisture, so the eggs will not dry out.

Detailed records are kept as to the mother, the number of eggs and how they were collected. Each egg is numbered, and the container is placed in an incubator that is programmed to maintain a specific temperature. In most species of turtles, the incubation temperature determines the gender of the hatchlings. It's important to incubate at a temperature that will produce both males and females.

Over the following days and weeks, the eggs must be watched carefully. Every few days, the container is weighed to see how much moisture has been lost, and water is added to return the moisture and humidity to the ideal level. This can take a long

time when a center is incubating a number of eggs!

Some of the eggs won't be fertile—meaning they will not hatch—but those that are healthy will start to hatch approximately two months after being laid.

Babies hatch without assistance, and once the yolk sac has been absorbed, the turtles are added to a shallow water set-up.

Egg containers must have water carefully added each week to ensure the right moisture for development.

Hatching and Release

The yolk sac on the baby's plastron is nature's way of providing nutrition while the baby is still in the nest.

atching time is exciting and very busy! After hatching, baby turtles have a "yolk sac" on their plastron region. This acts as a nutrition source for the first few days of their lives. The babies are allowed to absorb this until the whole sac disappears. Only then are they moved into the water.

In the wild, the turtles would move into the water on their own—a very dangerous journey—but in a center, the "clutch" of babies is kept together in a shallow water set-up, where they can start to move around and eat. Because turtles are cold-blooded, they must also be provided with a range of temperature options so they can choose what they need at different times. A heat light is set up so that there is always a nice, warm basking spot. An ultraviolet light is also provided, as reptiles are believed to depend on the sun's ultraviolet rays to activate vitamin D production, which in turn is responsible for allowing the absorption of calcium from the gastrointestinal tract.

Failing to provide the right diet, temperature, humidity and light will lead to deformities of the shell and poor growth.

The babies are released back into the environment that their mother came from.

Counterclockwise from top left:

Babies are added to a shallow water set-up in clutches. This is where they start to eat.

Many babies are released shortly after hatching.

Some babies are kept at the center longer.

Sea Turtles: A Special Case

Turtles that live in the sea cover large distances in their travels.

Sea turtles spend their life almost entirely in the water. But they must come onto the land to lay their eggs. This is usually done on beaches that are shared with humans. Many organizations and conservationists patrol these beaches nightly during the nesting season to protect the nests.

Sadly, the main predator is the human kind. Eggs are dug up by people and sold as food and medicine. Saving the eggs often comes down to a race between the poacher and the biologist!

If properly protected, sea turtle eggs incubate in the nest. When the eggs are "ready," the babies all emerge at the same time. They are tiny and can very easily fall prey to other animals on land and in the water. Left on their own, very few will make it to the often-massive size of their parents.

Marine turtle conservation organizations help to protect as many eggs and hatchlings as possible by educating the public. They teach people how to avoid nests, and about why it's important to turn off lights on the

beach at night (the lights can confuse the nesting females and the hatchlings). They also work to ensure that the hatchlings make it to the water.

Clockwise from top: Newly hatched turtles make their way to water as quickly as possible.

These eggs have just been laid on the beach.

Nest sites are marked with signs and warning tape so that people will stay away, and so biologists can monitor them.

So how do organizations dedicated to turtle conservation and rehabilitation know if their work is successful? Sometimes it's easy to tell: a turtle with a damaged shell comes in to a center, has its shell repaired and is returned to its home in the wild. Or perhaps the eggs of a deceased mother are harvested, incubated and hatched, saving a dozen unborn turtles from certain death.

Other times, though, it's not as easy to tell what needs to be done, or how best to do it. That's where field research and study come in. Field research is a natural extension of the work being done in a center, and it is essential to the conservation mission. Field research can involve many things, from tracking released headstarted turtles and performing population surveys to analyzing road mortalities and creating "ecopassages." Often, field research involves centers and organizations around the world working together on behalf of the turtles.

Going home: This adult snapping turtle is being released back into the wild—a satisfying part of field work.

Following the Headstarters

How do we know if a turtle species is at risk? Surveys help establish the health of an existing turtle population in a certain area and let conservationists know what efforts are needed. Population surveys are carried out in many ways—visual sightings, road mortality evaluations and "mark/recapture" studies where turtles are caught, identified with markings and then released again. To evaluate whether headstarting is an effective way to increase population size, the released juveniles are tracked via radio telemetry. A tiny radio transmitter is attached to the juvenile turtles' shells with epoxy. (The devices don't hurt the turtles in any way; they are less than 5 percent of the turtles' body weight.) Each transmitter has a unique frequency that can be detected by beeps on a receiver. Every week, the juveniles are located using this method. A group of wild juvenile turtles is followed at the same time, and the results are compared.

Why do we need to follow these turtles? First, scientists and

A "flipper tag" is sometimes used to identify individual marine turtles. The number is unique to that turtle, so the turtle can be identified if found, and its movements can be tracked.

Sharing Information

The Ontario Turtle Conservation Centre is involved in a large study with the support of the Ministry of Natural Resources' Species at Risk Stewardship Fund and also with funding from TD Friends of the Environment fund. This post-release study should provide good information that can be shared with conservationists around the world.

conservationists need to know whether headstarting programs are working. Do the babies survive? If they do not, we need to understand why. Are the turtles being released in the right place? What size should they be for the best chance of survival? Is there something that can be done differently?

We also need to know whether the released turtles are behaving in the same way as wild juveniles in the area. Are they eating what they should? Are they growing as they should? Are they hibernating successfully (and where are they hibernating)?

Top: Juvenile headstarted Blanding's turtles are tracked throughout the summer months. They are weighed and measured to assess how they are doing in the wild.

Bottom right: A "hoopnet" is placed to catch, mark and release wild Blanding's turtles in the same area. It allows us to compare our headstarted turtle's behaviour to their wild counterparts.

Bottom left: A swampy area is the favoured habitat for these juvenile Blanding's turtles. The antenna picks up the beep emitted from the transmitter, via a receiver. The location of the turtle can be pinpointed this way.

Protecting Turtles through Research

A baby snapping turtle: still legal to harvest for food.

The first step in introducing any kind of positive change is usually research. Before a problem can be fixed, it needs to be understood. Here are just a few examples of the field research taking place at turtle rescue and rehabilitation centers around the world.

Ecopassages

In North America and around the world, many problems occur when turtles try to cross roads. Signs that alert drivers to busy turtle crossing areas, and education to teach the public how to avoid turtles certainly help to prevent injuries and fatalities, but there's an even better solution: ecopassages. An ecopassage provides turtles with an alternative to a road crossing, such as an existing culvert under the road. "Exclusion fences" can be put up to help guide turtles to the culverts and away from danger. Much work is being done to establish the areas where ecopassages would be most effective, based on the information

Left: Fences lead the turtles toward the culverts, which provide safe passage under the road. Right: A camera has been mounted on this culvert to document the turtles using the ecopassage.

gathered when turtles are admitted to rehabilitation centers, and on ongoing mortality surveys.

The Plight of the Snapping Turtle

In 2011, the Ontario Turtle Trauma Centre partnered with the David Suzuki Foundation and Ontario Nature to help produce a report on the plight of the snapping turtle in Ontario. Although the snapping turtle is listed as a species of concern in the province, it is still legal to harvest these turtles for food. The OTCC conducted a study evaluating the levels of harmful mercury and PCB in turtle tissue. If people can't be convinced to stop hunting turtles for the turtle's sake, perhaps they will stop if they learn that snapping turtles are not safe to eat!

Colombian endemic river turtle

The Effects of Global Warming

Research is being carried out to determine the potential effects of global warming on turtle hatching. Because many species have temperature-dependent sex determination, a variation in climate conditions can affect the sex produced. A study has shown that the Colombian endemic river turtle, for example, has a limited ability to adapt to temperature change, and so is very vulnerable.

49

Nest protection and headstarting projects are underway in India, one of which aims to save the red-crowned roofed turtle (below).

Turtle Survival Alliance India

Turtle Survival Alliance India is headed by Shailendra Singh, who works tirelessly with his research crew to save the country's critically endangered turtles.

One of their projects involves a nest protection and headstarting program for the red-crowned roofed turtle. Nests are relocated to one central area, where they can be guarded night and day from poachers. The hatchlings are either released after hatching, or brought to TSA India's

facility in Madhya Pradesh (the Deori Eco-Centre) to be raised until their chances of survival will be increased. TSA India has recently started conducting a post-release study of these head-started turtles, tracking 10 individuals to determine survival. The organization also puts much emphasis on the education of local communities and prevention of poaching.

The Turtle Conservation Society of Malaysia

The Turtle Conservation Society of Malaysia, co-founded by Chan Eng Heng, carries out extensive field work and an ambitious education program. They have headstarted Southern River terrapins and released them into the Setiu River in Terengganu. The multi-year study evaluating the success of these headstarted turtles is showing great success. Their education program involves members of the community (of all ages). These local members are also integral to their headstarting program, housing the eggs and hatchlings at their homes.

Endangered in Madagascar

In Madagascar, ploughshare tortoises are critically endangered due to collection for the pet market. Collaboration between conservation and research organizations has led to field monitoring of the situation—conducting population surveys, collecting blood samples and screening for disease. Transmitters were placed on 23 wild tortoises. They will be tracked by local park patrolmen in Baly Bay to collect basic field data.

Working with the Enemy

Some former poachers of turtles have turned their skills toward conservation. Biologists realized that these individuals possessed unique skills in finding endangered turtles and their nests. They began to hire the poachers—making it more profitable to protect than poach. Sadly, many poachers still illegally take turtles and eggs from the wild in order to sell them. Educating the public not to buy these products—either for pets, food or medicine—is the key to taking away the market for illegally harvested turtles.

Chapter 6
Education and Conservation

If no one knows about the dire situation that turtles are in, nothing will change. Educating the public is perhaps the most important way that turtle rescue centers and conservation organizations can gain support. When people are aware of a problem, they can take steps to change it, and when many people take those steps together, change is much easier to achieve.

Education and conservation go hand in hand, with efforts in one area supporting efforts in another.

Education is vital to conservation efforts.

A Good Education

The People's Mosaic 2013

There are many ways to teach people about turtle conservation—school visits, education centers, adopt-a-turtle programs and even "turtle days."

World Turtle Day

Did you know that May 23 is World Turtle Day? Since 2000, the American Tortoise Rescue group has sponsored this global effort to increase knowledge of and respect for turtles, and to encourage people to help them survive and thrive. Turtle Day is celebrated in a many ways. Some people dress up as turtles or wear green clothes to show support. Others head to the highways to help turtles safely cross the road. Still others focus on research projects. There are even Turtle Day lesson plans and craft projects to help teachers talk about turtles in school classrooms.

Education Centers

Education centers provide great opportunities to work with the public. Rather than having a few

In India, they employ a unique education method—camels! The camel will be taken through various villages and will act as a portable billboard.

people travel all over to reach out to the community, the community can come to you. "Education turtles," like Andrea and Paddy (pictured at right), can be seen close up, allowing adults and children to really get to know the species we are trying to save. In addition, the public can see various parts of the hospital, including the surgery and laboratory, and the hatchling area.

Education through Art

At the Turtle Conservation Society of Malaysia, Chan Eng Heng painted an outdoor wall with murals depicting the plight of turtles. Turtle Alley, as its now called, highlights the fact that there that are more turtles and more turtle conservation work done in Terengganu than anywhere else in Peninsular Malaysia. Chan's original work has now been expanded to include more than 100 mosaics made and sponsored by visitors to the alley.

Education through Camel?

What if people can't come to a center? You take your education efforts on the road! In India, traveling by camel is an inventive way of making even the smallest villages aware of the threats that turtles face.

Turtle Teachers

Paddy is a snapping turtle who was raised by a family for 28 years. He cannot be released into the wild because we don't know where he originally came from. He has shown many people that snapping turtles don't need to be feared.

Paddy's "roommate" Andrea is a Blanding's turtle who is almost blind, and cannot be released back into the wild. She enjoys basking and hanging out in her own large pond, and is a favorite with the kids who come to the center.

Paddy the Blanding's turtle with his "roommate" Andrea.

Conservation: A Global Effort

A marine turtle undergoing treatment at the Loggerhead Marinelife Center in Juno Beach, Florida (inset).

Conservation efforts take place all around the world, all the time, and involve diverse members of the community. No matter your age, you can help.

Reintroducing the Radiated Tortoise

In Southern Madagascar, a community-based conservation program is working on behalf of the critically endangered radiated tortoise. This reintroduction program relies on public awareness and education to empower locals to protect wild tortoise populations and those released as part of the program. Without public support to prevent the causes of the population declines, a reintroduction program will not work.

Heading to the Beach

The Loggerhead Marinelife Center in Juno Beach, Florida, is one of many marine turtle conservation centers that protect nests and patrol beaches to prevent predation from poachers. On-site biologists evaluate the

success of hatching, and their education department carries out extensive outreach to teach locals what they can do to protect marine turtles.

Bringing Turtles Home

The Behler Chelonian Center in California recently carried out the first repatriation of the golden coin turtle, which is a critically endangered species found in China. These turtles were bred in captivity at the center and flown back "home" in 2013. They now form an important part of this newly introduced species.

New Efforts

In 2012, the Turtle Survival Alliance and the World Conservation Society joined forces to launch a new program in Colombia. Home to 27 species of turtles, Colombia is a key

Above left: The Behler Chelonian Center concentrates on breeding "assurance" colonies of endangered turtles and tortoises. These juvenile radiated tortoises were bred at the facility.

Above right: Radiated tortoise.

Below: Magdalena River turtle.

location for conservation in South America. One of the program's goals is to improve the country's zoos and rescue centers. Another is to support the conservation program for the threatened Magdalena River turtle.

Fighting Disease

Each fall, the human population worries about flu outbreaks, and everyone is encouraged to get a flu shot. Animals can be affected by outbreaks too. Ranavirus is a deadly DNA virus that can infect entire populations of amphibians, fish and reptiles. It has had such serious effects on populations that the Global Ranavirus Consortium was formed in 2011. Scientists and others world are working hard to learn more about the causes, prevention and treatment of this deadly disease.

Chapter 7

Get Involved

ow that you know about the threats that turtles face and the ways in which organizations around the world are trying to help, it's time for you to get involved.

Whether it's by helping a turtle to cross the road, lobbying for "turtle crossing" signs in your neighborhood or not buying turtles from the wild, you can make a difference.

Newly hatched baby sea turtles.

How to Help Turtles

The proper way to pick up a snapping turtle.

Hands-on Help

If you see a turtle on or about to cross the road, first make sure it is safe for you to help. If no cars are coming, you can help the turtle across the road in the direction they are going. Small turtles can safely be picked up by holding either side of the shell. Even little ones may bite if they are scared, so keep your fingers away from the mouth! When you see a snapping turtle on the road, it is best to get an adult to help you get him or her safely across the road. Keep your hands away from the front half of the body. Approach the turtle from behind, place your hand under their plastron and lift. They can snap quite quickly and their neck can come out quite far, so hold them away from the body.

Always wash your hands after handling a turtle, as they can sometimes have bacteria on their body.

Turtle Crossing

If you live in an area where turtles need to cross the road to get to their nesting areas or food sources, you

Turtle crossing signs do make a difference.

Volunteers from World Wildlife Fund helped out during OTCC's week-long spring field blitz.

can help by asking your local government to post "turtle crossing" signs. The Ontario Turtle Conservation Centre got its start when children in the Peterborough, Ontario, region became concerned about what they were seeing on the roads. They started the "Kids for Turtles" program to lobby for signs. Later, other people came on board and the center was formed. One child really can make a difference!

Volunteer

At the Ontario Turtle Conservation Centre, we welcome volunteers of all ages, as do many organizations like us. Children can volunteer with the supervision of their parents, and many also help with fundraisers to feed or treat a turtle. Some hold theme birthday parties, with participants donating to the turtle projects, while others may have bake sales or T-shirt sales. Still others hold larger fundraisers, and have even raised enough money to donate a microscope.

Turtles as Pets?

If you decide that you want a turtle as a pet, the best way to get one is through a facility that arranges adoptions of previously abandoned turtles. Remember, though, that turtles take a lot of specialized care to keep healthy. They require a lot of cleaning, and a lot of space—plus, they live a long, long time!

Learn More

There is so much good information out there about turtles, their lives and the ways in which they are threatened. If you want to learn more about the turtles in your area, or about a specific species that interests you, do some research! On page 63, you'll find a list of useful books, organizations and websites.

Glossary

Bycatch: anything caught unintentionally in fishing nets

Carapace: the upper portion of a turtle's shell

Cloaca: the single opening under a turtle's tail that is used for digestive, urinary and reproductive functions

Clutch: a group of eggs laid by a female at one time

Critically endangered: the International Union for Conservation of Nature (IUCN) has various levels of concern for species facing extinction; critically endangered is the highest risk for extinction in the near future

Ecotherms: animals that depend on the environment to maintain their body temperature; also known as "cold-blooded"

Endangered: the IUCN category just below "critically endangered"

Estivate: to spend the summer in a dormant state

Gravid: pregnant; carrying eggs or young

Habitat: an ecological or environmental area that is inhabited by a particular species of animal, plant or other type of organism

Headstarting: the act of artificially aiding in the incubating or raising of wildlife, to hopefully increase their chance of survival

Hibernate: to spend the winter in a dormant state

Incubate: to sit on eggs in order to keep them warm and bring them to hatching

Physiology: the way in which the various body systems work

Plastron: the lower portion of a turtle's shell

Radio telemetry: the act of following a wild animal by using a receiver that is programmed to detect a device attached to the animal

Scutes: the horny plates that cover a turtle's shell. They are made of living tissue and contain nerve endings, making it possible for turtles to feel when something touches their shell.

Second intention: the way in which a wound will heal if left to its own devices

Semi-aquatic: animals that divide their time between the water and the land

Vertebrates: Animals that have a backbone or spinal column—including mammals, fish, birds, reptiles and amphibians

Resources

United States

Marine Turtle Conservation Fund (U.S. Fish and Wildlife Service)
fws.gov/international/wildlife-without-borders/marine-turtle-conservation-fund.html

National Park Service Sea Turtle Conservation Program
nps.gov/bisc/naturescience/sea-turtle-conservation-program.htm

NOAA Fisheries Office of Protected Resources
www.nmfs.noaa.gov/pr/species/turtles

South Carolina Department of Natural Resources (SCDNR) Marine Turtle Conservation Program
dnr.sc.gov/seaturtle

Turtle Conservancy
turtleconservancy.org

Loggerhead Marinelife Center
marinelife.org

Sea Turtle Conservancy: Information About Sea Turtles, Their Habitats and Threats to Their Survival
conserveturtles.org

Seaworld
seaworldparks.com/en/seaworld-sandiego/animals/know-our-stars/sea-turtles/

Mote Marine Laboratory
mote.org

International

Littlefeet Environmental
littlefeet.org.uk

Turtle Survival Alliance (TSA operates globally with emphasis on Asia)
turtlesurvival.org

Turtle Conservation Society of Malaysia
turtleconservationsociety.org.my

Sea Turtle Conservation Bonaire
bonaireturtles.org

Turtle Farm (Tortugranja), Isla Mujeres, Mexico
soul-de-islamujeres.com/turtle-farm-isla-mujeres

Ontario Turtle Conservation Centre
kawarthaturtle.org

Environment Canada's Species at Risk Public Registry
sararegistry.gc.ca

Hinterland Who's Who — Species at Risk in Canada
hww.ca

Nova Scotia Leatherbacks
seaturtle.ca

Conservation International
conservationorg/learn/biodiversity/species/profiles/turtles/pages/turtles.aspx

Seeturtles
seeturtles.org

Index